Pet S...

Logbook and Scheduler

Logbook Year: _____

Logbook Number: _____

Table of Contents

Client Name	Phone	Page

Month:

Date:	MONDAY	TUESDAY	WEDNESDAY	THURSDAY	FRIDAY	SATURDAY	SUNDAY
5:00							
5:30							
6:00							
6:30							
7:00							
7:30							
8:00							
8:30							

Pet Name:

Owner

Name:

Address:

Email: | Emergency:

Veterinarian

Name: | Phone:

Act Immediately in Emergency: ☐   Contact Owners First: ☐

Pet Info

Nickname: | Age & Gender:

Species: | Breed:

Hiding Places: | Favorite Toy:

Allergies: | Favorite Treat:

Meals

Time: | Meal: | Quantity:

Time: | Meal: | Quantity:

Time: | Meal: | Quantity:

Other

Walk: ☐   Groom: ☐   Play: ☐   Clean Litter: ☐   Other:

Billing

Fee Per Visit:	Visits:	Visit Total:
Extra Fees:	Discounts:	Extras Total:
Paid?	Method:	TOTAL:

Notes

Life Books

Usage Tips

We're so glad you've decided to use our Pet Sitter log book! You should use it whatever way works best for you, but we wanted to give a few suggestions to get you started.

If you love our book, we'd *really* appreciate an honest review on Amazon. It helps a us a *lot*! 💙

Table of Contents / Index

- It can be helpful to use the Pet name as the Client name
- If clients have more than one pet, add a line for *each pet*!
- Try to keep all of a client's pets on consecutive lines

Client Information

- Use the information you need to fill out this section as an on-boarding questionnaire for your clients
- If a client gives too much information to fit on the page, use the Notes section to note a page number in the *book* notes section, where you can put the rest of the information

Notes

- This section is ideal for making notes about clients that there wasn't room for on the main page, but make sure to add page numbers to the relevant client so that you can find them again!
- It's a good idea to keep track of how pets behaved, if they were unfriendly, seemed sick, or anything else odd
- It's also a good idea to make notes about owner behavior!

52 Weeks At a Glance

- In the Date above the Days, write the day number of the month (e.g. 17th)
- If you have big handwriting, write a Page Number rather than a name in the day/time space

Table of Contents

Client Name	Phone	Page

Client Name	Phone	Page

Client Name	Phone	Page

Pet Name:

Owner

Name:

Address:

Email:	Emergency:

Veterinarian

Name:	Phone:

Act Immediately in Emergency: ☐   Contact Owners First: ☐

Pet Info

Nickname:	Age & Gender:
Species:	Breed:
Hiding Places:	Favorite Toy:
Allergies:	Favorite Treat:

Meals

Time:	Meal:	Quantity:
Time:	Meal:	Quantity:
Time:	Meal:	Quantity:

Other

Walk: ☐   Groom: ☐   Play: ☐   Clean Litter: ☐   Other:

Billing

Fee Per Visit:	Visits:	Visit Total:
Extra Fees:	Discounts:	Extras Total:
Paid?	Method:	**TOTAL:**

Notes

Pet Name:

Owner

Name:	
Address:	
Email:	Emergency:

Veterinarian

Name:	Phone:
Act Immediately in Emergency: ☐	Contact Owners First: ☐

Pet Info

Nickname:	Age & Gender:
Species:	Breed:
Hiding Places:	Favorite Toy:
Allergies:	Favorite Treat:

Meals

Time:	Meal:	Quantity:
Time:	Meal:	Quantity:
Time:	Meal:	Quantity:

Other

Walk: ☐   Groom: ☐   Play: ☐   Clean Litter: ☐   Other:

Billing

Fee Per Visit:	Visits:	Visit Total:
Extra Fees:	Discounts:	Extras Total:
Paid?	Method:	**TOTAL:**

Notes

Pet Name:

Owner

Name:	
Address:	
Email:	Emergency:

Veterinarian

Name:	Phone:
Act Immediately in Emergency: ☐	Contact Owners First: ☐

Pet Info

Nickname:	Age & Gender:
Species:	Breed:
Hiding Places:	Favorite Toy:
Allergies:	Favorite Treat:

Meals

Time:	Meal:	Quantity:
Time:	Meal:	Quantity:
Time:	Meal:	Quantity:

Other

Walk: ☐   Groom: ☐   Play: ☐   Clean Litter: ☐   Other:

Billing

Fee Per Visit:	Visits:	Visit Total:
Extra Fees:	Discounts:	Extras Total:
Paid?	Method:	**TOTAL:**

Notes

_____
_____
_____

Pet Name:

Owner

Name:	
Address:	
Email:	Emergency:

Veterinarian

Name:	Phone:
Act Immediately in Emergency: ☐	Contact Owners First: ☐

Pet Info

Nickname:	Age & Gender:
Species:	Breed:
Hiding Places:	Favorite Toy:
Allergies:	Favorite Treat:

Meals

Time:	Meal:	Quantity:
Time:	Meal:	Quantity:
Time:	Meal:	Quantity:

Other

Walk: ☐   Groom: ☐   Play: ☐   Clean Litter: ☐   Other:

Billing

Fee Per Visit:	Visits:	Visit Total:
Extra Fees:	Discounts:	Extras Total:
Paid?	Method:	**TOTAL:**

Notes

Pet Name:

Owner

Name:	
Address:	
Email:	Emergency:

Veterinarian

Name:	Phone:
Act Immediately in Emergency: ☐	Contact Owners First: ☐

Pet Info

Nickname:	Age & Gender:
Species:	Breed:
Hiding Places:	Favorite Toy:
Allergies:	Favorite Treat:

Meals

Time:	Meal:	Quantity:
Time:	Meal:	Quantity:
Time:	Meal:	Quantity:

Other

Walk: ☐   Groom: ☐   Play: ☐   Clean Litter: ☐   Other:

Billing

Fee Per Visit:	Visits:	Visit Total:
Extra Fees:	Discounts:	Extras Total:
Paid?	Method:	**TOTAL:**

Notes

_____

_____

_____

Pet Name:

Owner

Name:	
Address:	
Email:	Emergency:

Veterinarian

Name:	Phone:
Act Immediately in Emergency: ☐	Contact Owners First: ☐

Pet Info

Nickname:	Age & Gender:
Species:	Breed:
Hiding Places:	Favorite Toy:
Allergies:	Favorite Treat:

Meals

Time:	Meal:	Quantity:
Time:	Meal:	Quantity:
Time:	Meal:	Quantity:

Other

Walk: ☐   Groom: ☐   Play: ☐   Clean Litter: ☐   Other:

Billing

Fee Per Visit:	Visits:	Visit Total:
Extra Fees:	Discounts:	Extras Total:
Paid?	Method:	**TOTAL:**

Notes

Pet Name:

Owner

Name:	
Address:	
Email:	Emergency:

Veterinarian

Name:	Phone:
Act Immediately in Emergency: ☐	Contact Owners First: ☐

Pet Info

Nickname:	Age & Gender:
Species:	Breed:
Hiding Places:	Favorite Toy:
Allergies:	Favorite Treat:

Meals

Time:	Meal:	Quantity:
Time:	Meal:	Quantity:
Time:	Meal:	Quantity:

Other

Walk: ☐ Groom: ☐ Play: ☐ Clean Litter: ☐ Other:

Billing

Fee Per Visit:	Visits:	Visit Total:
Extra Fees:	Discounts:	Extras Total:
Paid?	Method:	**TOTAL:**

Notes

_____

_____

_____

Pet Name:

Owner

Name:	
Address:	
Email:	Emergency:

Veterinarian

Name:	Phone:
Act Immediately in Emergency: ☐	Contact Owners First: ☐

Pet Info

Nickname:	Age & Gender:
Species:	Breed:
Hiding Places:	Favorite Toy:
Allergies:	Favorite Treat:

Meals

Time:	Meal:	Quantity:
Time:	Meal:	Quantity:
Time:	Meal:	Quantity:

Other

Walk: ☐   Groom: ☐   Play: ☐   Clean Litter: ☐   Other:

Billing

Fee Per Visit:	Visits:	Visit Total:
Extra Fees:	Discounts:	Extras Total:
Paid?	Method:	**TOTAL:**

Notes

Pet Name:

Owner

Name:	
Address:	
Email:	Emergency:

Veterinarian

Name:	Phone:
Act Immediately in Emergency: ☐	Contact Owners First: ☐

Pet Info

Nickname:	Age & Gender:
Species:	Breed:
Hiding Places:	Favorite Toy:
Allergies:	Favorite Treat:

Meals

Time:	Meal:	Quantity:
Time:	Meal:	Quantity:
Time:	Meal:	Quantity:

Other

Walk: ☐   Groom: ☐   Play: ☐   Clean Litter: ☐   Other:

Billing

Fee Per Visit:	Visits:	Visit Total:
Extra Fees:	Discounts:	Extras Total:
Paid?	Method:	**TOTAL:**

Notes

_____

_____

_____

Pet Name:

Owner

Name:	
Address:	
Email:	Emergency:

Veterinarian

Name:	Phone:

Act Immediately in Emergency: ☐   Contact Owners First: ☐

Pet Info

Nickname:	Age & Gender:
Species:	Breed:
Hiding Places:	Favorite Toy:
Allergies:	Favorite Treat:

Meals

Time:	Meal:	Quantity:
Time:	Meal:	Quantity:
Time:	Meal:	Quantity:

Other

Walk: ☐   Groom: ☐   Play: ☐   Clean Litter: ☐   Other:

Billing

Fee Per Visit:	Visits:	Visit Total:
Extra Fees:	Discounts:	Extras Total:
Paid?	Method:	**TOTAL:**

Notes

Pet Name:

Owner

Name:	
Address:	
Email:	Emergency:

Veterinarian

Name:	Phone:
Act Immediately in Emergency: ☐	Contact Owners First: ☐

Pet Info

Nickname:	Age & Gender:
Species:	Breed:
Hiding Places:	Favorite Toy:
Allergies:	Favorite Treat:

Meals

Time:	Meal:	Quantity:
Time:	Meal:	Quantity:
Time:	Meal:	Quantity:

Other

Walk: ☐   Groom: ☐   Play: ☐   Clean Litter: ☐   Other:

Billing

Fee Per Visit:	Visits:	Visit Total:
Extra Fees:	Discounts:	Extras Total:
Paid?	Method:	**TOTAL:**

Notes

_____

_____

_____

Pet Name:

Owner

Name:	
Address:	
Email:	Emergency:

Veterinarian

Name:	Phone:

Act Immediately in Emergency: ☐   Contact Owners First: ☐

Pet Info

Nickname:	Age & Gender:
Species:	Breed:
Hiding Places:	Favorite Toy:
Allergies:	Favorite Treat:

Meals

Time:	Meal:	Quantity:
Time:	Meal:	Quantity:
Time:	Meal:	Quantity:

Other

Walk: ☐   Groom: ☐   Play: ☐   Clean Litter: ☐   Other:

Billing

Fee Per Visit:	Visits:	Visit Total:
Extra Fees:	Discounts:	Extras Total:
Paid?	Method:	**TOTAL:**

Notes

Pet Name:

Owner

Name:	
Address:	
Email:	Emergency:

Veterinarian

Name:	Phone:
Act Immediately in Emergency: ☐	Contact Owners First: ☐

Pet Info

Nickname:	Age & Gender:
Species:	Breed:
Hiding Places:	Favorite Toy:
Allergies:	Favorite Treat:

Meals

Time:	Meal:	Quantity:
Time:	Meal:	Quantity:
Time:	Meal:	Quantity:

Other

Walk: ☐   Groom: ☐   Play: ☐   Clean Litter: ☐   Other:

Billing

Fee Per Visit:	Visits:	Visit Total:
Extra Fees:	Discounts:	Extras Total:
Paid?	Method:	**TOTAL:**

Notes

_____
_____
_____

Pet Name:

Owner

Name:	
Address:	
Email:	Emergency:

Veterinarian

Name:	Phone:
Act Immediately in Emergency: ☐	Contact Owners First: ☐

Pet Info

Nickname:	Age & Gender:
Species:	Breed:
Hiding Places:	Favorite Toy:
Allergies:	Favorite Treat:

Meals

Time:	Meal:	Quantity:
Time:	Meal:	Quantity:
Time:	Meal:	Quantity:

Other

Walk: ☐   Groom: ☐   Play: ☐   Clean Litter: ☐   Other:

Billing

Fee Per Visit:	Visits:	Visit Total:
Extra Fees:	Discounts:	Extras Total:
Paid?	Method:	**TOTAL:**

Notes

Pet Name:

Owner

Name:	
Address:	
Email:	Emergency:

Veterinarian

Name:	Phone:
Act Immediately in Emergency: ☐	Contact Owners First: ☐

Pet Info

Nickname:	Age & Gender:
Species:	Breed:
Hiding Places:	Favorite Toy:
Allergies:	Favorite Treat:

Meals

Time:	Meal:	Quantity:
Time:	Meal:	Quantity:
Time:	Meal:	Quantity:

Other

Walk: ☐   Groom: ☐   Play: ☐   Clean Litter: ☐   Other:

Billing

Fee Per Visit:	Visits:	Visit Total:
Extra Fees:	Discounts:	Extras Total:
Paid?	Method:	**TOTAL:**

Notes

Pet Name:

Owner

Name:	
Address:	
Email:	Emergency:

Veterinarian

Name:	Phone:
Act Immediately in Emergency: ☐	Contact Owners First: ☐

Pet Info

Nickname:	Age & Gender:
Species:	Breed:
Hiding Places:	Favorite Toy:
Allergies:	Favorite Treat:

Meals

Time:	Meal:	Quantity:
Time:	Meal:	Quantity:
Time:	Meal:	Quantity:

Other

Walk: ☐   Groom: ☐   Play: ☐   Clean Litter: ☐   Other:

Billing

Fee Per Visit:	Visits:	Visit Total:
Extra Fees:	Discounts:	Extras Total:
Paid?	Method:	**TOTAL:**

Notes

Pet Name:

Owner

Name:	
Address:	
Email:	Emergency:

Veterinarian

Name:	Phone:
Act Immediately in Emergency: ☐	Contact Owners First: ☐

Pet Info

Nickname:	Age & Gender:
Species:	Breed:
Hiding Places:	Favorite Toy:
Allergies:	Favorite Treat:

Meals

Time:	Meal:	Quantity:
Time:	Meal:	Quantity:
Time:	Meal:	Quantity:

Other

Walk: ☐   Groom: ☐   Play: ☐   Clean Litter: ☐   Other:

Billing

Fee Per Visit:	Visits:	Visit Total:
Extra Fees:	Discounts:	Extras Total:
Paid?	Method:	**TOTAL:**

Notes

_____

_____

_____

Pet Name:

Owner

Name:	
Address:	
Email:	Emergency:

Veterinarian

Name:	Phone:

Act Immediately in Emergency: ☐   Contact Owners First: ☐

Pet Info

Nickname:	Age & Gender:
Species:	Breed:
Hiding Places:	Favorite Toy:
Allergies:	Favorite Treat:

Meals

Time:	Meal:	Quantity:
Time:	Meal:	Quantity:
Time:	Meal:	Quantity:

Other

Walk: ☐   Groom: ☐   Play: ☐   Clean Litter: ☐   Other:

Billing

Fee Per Visit:	Visits:	Visit Total:
Extra Fees:	Discounts:	Extras Total:
Paid?	Method:	**TOTAL:**

Notes

Pet Name:

Owner

Name:	
Address:	
Email:	Emergency:

Veterinarian

Name:	Phone:
Act Immediately in Emergency: ☐	Contact Owners First: ☐

Pet Info

Nickname:	Age & Gender:
Species:	Breed:
Hiding Places:	Favorite Toy:
Allergies:	Favorite Treat:

Meals

Time:	Meal:	Quantity:
Time:	Meal:	Quantity:
Time:	Meal:	Quantity:

Other

Walk: ☐   Groom: ☐   Play: ☐   Clean Litter: ☐   Other:

Billing

Fee Per Visit:	Visits:	Visit Total:
Extra Fees:	Discounts:	Extras Total:
Paid?	Method:	**TOTAL:**

Notes

_____
_____
_____

Pet Name:

Owner

Name:	
Address:	
Email:	Emergency:

Veterinarian

Name:	Phone:
Act Immediately in Emergency: ☐	Contact Owners First: ☐

Pet Info

Nickname:	Age & Gender:
Species:	Breed:
Hiding Places:	Favorite Toy:
Allergies:	Favorite Treat:

Meals

Time:	Meal:	Quantity:
Time:	Meal:	Quantity:
Time:	Meal:	Quantity:

Other

Walk: ☐   Groom: ☐   Play: ☐   Clean Litter: ☐   Other:

Billing

Fee Per Visit:	Visits:	Visit Total:
Extra Fees:	Discounts:	Extras Total:
Paid?	Method:	**TOTAL:**

Notes

Pet Name:

Owner

Name:	
Address:	
Email:	Emergency:

Veterinarian

Name:	Phone:
Act Immediately in Emergency: ☐	Contact Owners First: ☐

Pet Info

Nickname:	Age & Gender:
Species:	Breed:
Hiding Places:	Favorite Toy:
Allergies:	Favorite Treat:

Meals

Time:	Meal:	Quantity:
Time:	Meal:	Quantity:
Time:	Meal:	Quantity:

Other

Walk: ☐   Groom: ☐   Play: ☐   Clean Litter: ☐   Other:

Billing

Fee Per Visit:	Visits:	Visit Total:
Extra Fees:	Discounts:	Extras Total:
Paid?	Method:	**TOTAL:**

Notes

_____

_____

_____

Pet Name:

Owner

Name:	
Address:	
Email:	Emergency:

Veterinarian

Name:	Phone:
Act Immediately in Emergency: ☐	Contact Owners First: ☐

Pet Info

Nickname:	Age & Gender:
Species:	Breed:
Hiding Places:	Favorite Toy:
Allergies:	Favorite Treat:

Meals

Time:	Meal:	Quantity:
Time:	Meal:	Quantity:
Time:	Meal:	Quantity:

Other

Walk: ☐   Groom: ☐   Play: ☐   Clean Litter: ☐   Other:

Billing

Fee Per Visit:	Visits:	Visit Total:
Extra Fees:	Discounts:	Extras Total:
Paid?	Method:	**TOTAL:**

Notes

_____

_____

_____

Pet Name:

Owner

Name:	
Address:	
Email:	Emergency:

Veterinarian

Name:	Phone:
Act Immediately in Emergency: ☐	Contact Owners First: ☐

Pet Info

Nickname:	Age & Gender:
Species:	Breed:
Hiding Places:	Favorite Toy:
Allergies:	Favorite Treat:

Meals

Time:	Meal:	Quantity:
Time:	Meal:	Quantity:
Time:	Meal:	Quantity:

Other

Walk: ☐   Groom: ☐   Play: ☐   Clean Litter: ☐   Other:

Billing

Fee Per Visit:	Visits:	Visit Total:
Extra Fees:	Discounts:	Extras Total:
Paid?	Method:	**TOTAL:**

Notes

_____
_____
_____

Pet Name:

Owner

Name:

Address:

Email:	Emergency:

Veterinarian

Name:	Phone:

Act Immediately in Emergency: ☐   Contact Owners First: ☐

Pet Info

Nickname:	Age & Gender:
Species:	Breed:
Hiding Places:	Favorite Toy:
Allergies:	Favorite Treat:

Meals

Time:	Meal:	Quantity:
Time:	Meal:	Quantity:
Time:	Meal:	Quantity:

Other

Walk: ☐   Groom: ☐   Play: ☐   Clean Litter: ☐   Other:

Billing

Fee Per Visit:	Visits:	Visit Total:
Extra Fees:	Discounts:	Extras Total:
Paid?	Method:	**TOTAL:**

Notes

_____

_____

_____

_____

Pet Name:

Owner

Name:	
Address:	
Email:	Emergency:

Veterinarian

Name:	Phone:
Act Immediately in Emergency: ☐	Contact Owners First: ☐

Pet Info

Nickname:	Age & Gender:
Species:	Breed:
Hiding Places:	Favorite Toy:
Allergies:	Favorite Treat:

Meals

Time:	Meal:	Quantity:
Time:	Meal:	Quantity:
Time:	Meal:	Quantity:

Other

Walk: ☐   Groom: ☐   Play: ☐   Clean Litter: ☐   Other:

Billing

Fee Per Visit:	Visits:	Visit Total:
Extra Fees:	Discounts:	Extras Total:
Paid?	Method:	**TOTAL:**

Notes

Pet Name:

Owner

Name:	
Address:	
Email:	Emergency:

Veterinarian

Name:	Phone:

Act Immediately in Emergency: ☐　　Contact Owners First: ☐

Pet Info

Nickname:	Age & Gender:
Species:	Breed:
Hiding Places:	Favorite Toy:
Allergies:	Favorite Treat:

Meals

Time:	Meal:	Quantity:
Time:	Meal:	Quantity:
Time:	Meal:	Quantity:

Other

Walk: ☐　　Groom: ☐　　Play: ☐　　Clean Litter: ☐　　Other:

Billing

Fee Per Visit:	Visits:	Visit Total:
Extra Fees:	Discounts:	Extras Total:
Paid?	Method:	**TOTAL:**

Notes

Pet Name:

Owner

Name:	
Address:	
Email:	Emergency:

Veterinarian

Name:	Phone:
Act Immediately in Emergency: ☐	Contact Owners First: ☐

Pet Info

Nickname:	Age & Gender:
Species:	Breed:
Hiding Places:	Favorite Toy:
Allergies:	Favorite Treat:

Meals

Time:	Meal:	Quantity:
Time:	Meal:	Quantity:
Time:	Meal:	Quantity:

Other

Walk: ☐   Groom: ☐   Play: ☐   Clean Litter: ☐   Other:

Billing

Fee Per Visit:	Visits:	Visit Total:
Extra Fees:	Discounts:	Extras Total:
Paid?	Method:	**TOTAL:**

Notes

_____

_____

_____

Pet Name:

Owner

Name:

Address:

Email:	Emergency:

Veterinarian

Name:	Phone:

Act Immediately in Emergency: ☐   Contact Owners First: ☐

Pet Info

Nickname:	Age & Gender:
Species:	Breed:
Hiding Places:	Favorite Toy:
Allergies:	Favorite Treat:

Meals

Time:	Meal:	Quantity:
Time:	Meal:	Quantity:
Time:	Meal:	Quantity:

Other

Walk: ☐   Groom: ☐   Play: ☐   Clean Litter: ☐   Other:

Billing

Fee Per Visit:	Visits:	Visit Total:
Extra Fees:	Discounts:	Extras Total:
Paid?	Method:	**TOTAL:**

Notes

Pet Name:

Owner

Name:	
Address:	
Email:	Emergency:

Veterinarian

Name:	Phone:
Act Immediately in Emergency: ☐	Contact Owners First: ☐

Pet Info

Nickname:	Age & Gender:
Species:	Breed:
Hiding Places:	Favorite Toy:
Allergies:	Favorite Treat:

Meals

Time:	Meal:	Quantity:
Time:	Meal:	Quantity:
Time:	Meal:	Quantity:

Other

Walk: ☐   Groom: ☐   Play: ☐   Clean Litter: ☐   Other:

Billing

Fee Per Visit:	Visits:	Visit Total:
Extra Fees:	Discounts:	Extras Total:
Paid?	Method:	**TOTAL:**

Notes

Pet Name:

Owner

Name:	
Address:	
Email:	Emergency:

Veterinarian

Name:	Phone:
Act Immediately in Emergency: ☐	Contact Owners First: ☐

Pet Info

Nickname:	Age & Gender:
Species:	Breed:
Hiding Places:	Favorite Toy:
Allergies:	Favorite Treat:

Meals

Time:	Meal:	Quantity:
Time:	Meal:	Quantity:
Time:	Meal:	Quantity:

Other

Walk: ☐   Groom: ☐   Play: ☐   Clean Litter: ☐   Other:

Billing

Fee Per Visit:	Visits:	Visit Total:
Extra Fees:	Discounts:	Extras Total:
Paid?	Method:	**TOTAL:**

Notes

Pet Name:

Owner

Name:

Address:

Email: | Emergency:

Veterinarian

Name: | Phone:

Act Immediately in Emergency: ☐   Contact Owners First: ☐

Pet Info

Nickname: | Age & Gender:

Species: | Breed:

Hiding Places: | Favorite Toy:

Allergies: | Favorite Treat:

Meals

Time:	Meal:	Quantity:
Time:	Meal:	Quantity:
Time:	Meal:	Quantity:

Other

Walk: ☐   Groom: ☐   Play: ☐   Clean Litter: ☐   Other:

Billing

Fee Per Visit:	Visits:	Visit Total:
Extra Fees:	Discounts:	Extras Total:
Paid?	Method:	**TOTAL:**

Notes

Pet Name:

Owner

Name:

Address:

Email:	Emergency:

Veterinarian

Name:	Phone:

Act Immediately in Emergency: ☐   Contact Owners First: ☐

Pet Info

Nickname:	Age & Gender:
Species:	Breed:
Hiding Places:	Favorite Toy:
Allergies:	Favorite Treat:

Meals

Time:	Meal:	Quantity:
Time:	Meal:	Quantity:
Time:	Meal:	Quantity:

Other

Walk: ☐   Groom: ☐   Play: ☐   Clean Litter: ☐   Other:

Billing

Fee Per Visit:	Visits:	Visit Total:
Extra Fees:	Discounts:	Extras Total:
Paid?	Method:	**TOTAL:**

Notes

_____

_____

_____

_____

Pet Name:

Owner

Name:	
Address:	
Email:	Emergency:

Veterinarian

Name:	Phone:
Act Immediately in Emergency: ☐	Contact Owners First: ☐

Pet Info

Nickname:	Age & Gender:
Species:	Breed:
Hiding Places:	Favorite Toy:
Allergies:	Favorite Treat:

Meals

Time:	Meal:	Quantity:
Time:	Meal:	Quantity:
Time:	Meal:	Quantity:

Other

Walk: ☐   Groom: ☐   Play: ☐   Clean Litter: ☐   Other:

Billing

Fee Per Visit:	Visits:	Visit Total:
Extra Fees:	Discounts:	Extras Total:
Paid?	Method:	**TOTAL:**

Notes

Pet Name:

Owner

Name:	
Address:	
Email:	Emergency:

Veterinarian

Name:	Phone:
Act Immediately in Emergency: ☐	Contact Owners First: ☐

Pet Info

Nickname:	Age & Gender:
Species:	Breed:
Hiding Places:	Favorite Toy:
Allergies:	Favorite Treat:

Meals

Time:	Meal:	Quantity:
Time:	Meal:	Quantity:
Time:	Meal:	Quantity:

Other

Walk: ☐   Groom: ☐   Play: ☐   Clean Litter: ☐   Other:

Billing

Fee Per Visit:	Visits:	Visit Total:
Extra Fees:	Discounts:	Extras Total:
Paid?	Method:	**TOTAL:**

Notes

Pet Name:

Owner

Name:	
Address:	
Email:	Emergency:

Veterinarian

Name:	Phone:
Act Immediately in Emergency: ☐	Contact Owners First: ☐

Pet Info

Nickname:	Age & Gender:
Species:	Breed:
Hiding Places:	Favorite Toy:
Allergies:	Favorite Treat:

Meals

Time:	Meal:	Quantity:
Time:	Meal:	Quantity:
Time:	Meal:	Quantity:

Other

Walk: ☐   Groom: ☐   Play: ☐   Clean Litter: ☐   Other:

Billing

Fee Per Visit:	Visits:	Visit Total:
Extra Fees:	Discounts:	Extras Total:
Paid?	Method:	**TOTAL:**

Notes

_____
_____
_____

Pet Name:

Owner

Name:	
Address:	
Email:	Emergency:

Veterinarian

Name:	Phone:

Act Immediately in Emergency: ☐   Contact Owners First: ☐

Pet Info

Nickname:	Age & Gender:
Species:	Breed:
Hiding Places:	Favorite Toy:
Allergies:	Favorite Treat:

Meals

Time:	Meal:	Quantity:
Time:	Meal:	Quantity:
Time:	Meal:	Quantity:

Other

Walk: ☐   Groom: ☐   Play: ☐   Clean Litter: ☐   Other:

Billing

Fee Per Visit:	Visits:	Visit Total:
Extra Fees:	Discounts:	Extras Total:
Paid?	Method:	**TOTAL:**

Notes

Pet Name:

Owner

Name:	
Address:	
Email:	Emergency:

Veterinarian

Name:	Phone:
Act Immediately in Emergency: ☐	Contact Owners First: ☐

Pet Info

Nickname:	Age & Gender:
Species:	Breed:
Hiding Places:	Favorite Toy:
Allergies:	Favorite Treat:

Meals

Time:	Meal:	Quantity:
Time:	Meal:	Quantity:
Time:	Meal:	Quantity:

Other

Walk: ☐   Groom: ☐   Play: ☐   Clean Litter: ☐   Other:

Billing

Fee Per Visit:	Visits:	Visit Total:
Extra Fees:	Discounts:	Extras Total:
Paid?	Method:	**TOTAL:**

Notes

_____
_____
_____

Pet Name:

Owner

Name:

Address:

Email: | Emergency:

Veterinarian

Name: | Phone:

Act Immediately in Emergency: ☐   Contact Owners First: ☐

Pet Info

Nickname:	Age & Gender:
Species:	Breed:
Hiding Places:	Favorite Toy:
Allergies:	Favorite Treat:

Meals

Time:	Meal:	Quantity:
Time:	Meal:	Quantity:
Time:	Meal:	Quantity:

Other

Walk: ☐   Groom: ☐   Play: ☐   Clean Litter: ☐   Other:

Billing

Fee Per Visit:	Visits:	Visit Total:
Extra Fees:	Discounts:	Extras Total:
Paid?	Method:	**TOTAL:**

Notes

Pet Name:

Owner

Name:	
Address:	
Email:	Emergency:

Veterinarian

Name:	Phone:
Act Immediately in Emergency: ☐	Contact Owners First: ☐

Pet Info

Nickname:	Age & Gender:
Species:	Breed:
Hiding Places:	Favorite Toy:
Allergies:	Favorite Treat:

Meals

Time:	Meal:	Quantity:
Time:	Meal:	Quantity:
Time:	Meal:	Quantity:

Other

Walk: ☐   Groom: ☐   Play: ☐   Clean Litter: ☐   Other:

Billing

Fee Per Visit:	Visits:	Visit Total:
Extra Fees:	Discounts:	Extras Total:
Paid?	Method:	**TOTAL:**

Notes

_____
_____
_____

Pet Name:

Owner

Name:

Address:

Email: | Emergency:

Veterinarian

Name: | Phone:

Act Immediately in Emergency: ☐   Contact Owners First: ☐

Pet Info

Nickname:	Age & Gender:
Species:	Breed:
Hiding Places:	Favorite Toy:
Allergies:	Favorite Treat:

Meals

Time:	Meal:	Quantity:
Time:	Meal:	Quantity:
Time:	Meal:	Quantity:

Other

Walk: ☐   Groom: ☐   Play: ☐   Clean Litter: ☐   Other:

Billing

Fee Per Visit:	Visits:	Visit Total:
Extra Fees:	Discounts:	Extras Total:
Paid?	Method:	**TOTAL:**

Notes

Pet Name:

Owner

Name:	
Address:	
Email:	Emergency:

Veterinarian

Name:	Phone:
Act Immediately in Emergency: ☐	Contact Owners First: ☐

Pet Info

Nickname:	Age & Gender:
Species:	Breed:
Hiding Places:	Favorite Toy:
Allergies:	Favorite Treat:

Meals

Time:	Meal:	Quantity:
Time:	Meal:	Quantity:
Time:	Meal:	Quantity:

Other

Walk: ☐   Groom: ☐   Play: ☐   Clean Litter: ☐   Other:

Billing

Fee Per Visit:	Visits:	Visit Total:
Extra Fees:	Discounts:	Extras Total:
Paid?	Method:	**TOTAL:**

Notes

Pet Name:

Owner

Name:	
Address:	
Email:	Emergency:

Veterinarian

Name:	Phone:
Act Immediately in Emergency: ☐	Contact Owners First: ☐

Pet Info

Nickname:	Age & Gender:
Species:	Breed:
Hiding Places:	Favorite Toy:
Allergies:	Favorite Treat:

Meals

Time:	Meal:	Quantity:
Time:	Meal:	Quantity:
Time:	Meal:	Quantity:

Other

Walk: ☐   Groom: ☐   Play: ☐   Clean Litter: ☐   Other:

Billing

Fee Per Visit:	Visits:	Visit Total:
Extra Fees:	Discounts:	Extras Total:
Paid?	Method:	**TOTAL:**

Notes

Pet Name:

Owner

Name:	
Address:	
Email:	Emergency:

Veterinarian

Name:	Phone:
Act Immediately in Emergency: ☐	Contact Owners First: ☐

Pet Info

Nickname:	Age & Gender:
Species:	Breed:
Hiding Places:	Favorite Toy:
Allergies:	Favorite Treat:

Meals

Time:	Meal:	Quantity:
Time:	Meal:	Quantity:
Time:	Meal:	Quantity:

Other

Walk: ☐   Groom: ☐   Play: ☐   Clean Litter: ☐   Other:

Billing

Fee Per Visit:	Visits:	Visit Total:
Extra Fees:	Discounts:	Extras Total:
Paid?	Method:	**TOTAL:**

Notes

_____
_____
_____
_____

Pet Name:

Owner

Name:	
Address:	
Email:	Emergency:

Veterinarian

Name:	Phone:
Act Immediately in Emergency: ☐	Contact Owners First: ☐

Pet Info

Nickname:	Age & Gender:
Species:	Breed:
Hiding Places:	Favorite Toy:
Allergies:	Favorite Treat:

Meals

Time:	Meal:	Quantity:
Time:	Meal:	Quantity:
Time:	Meal:	Quantity:

Other

Walk: ☐   Groom: ☐   Play: ☐   Clean Litter: ☐   Other:

Billing

Fee Per Visit:	Visits:	Visit Total:
Extra Fees:	Discounts:	Extras Total:
Paid?	Method:	**TOTAL:**

Notes

_____
_____
_____
_____

Pet Name:

Owner

Name:	
Address:	
Email:	Emergency:

Veterinarian

Name:	Phone:
Act Immediately in Emergency: ☐	Contact Owners First: ☐

Pet Info

Nickname:	Age & Gender:
Species:	Breed:
Hiding Places:	Favorite Toy:
Allergies:	Favorite Treat:

Meals

Time:	Meal:	Quantity:
Time:	Meal:	Quantity:
Time:	Meal:	Quantity:

Other

Walk: ☐   Groom: ☐   Play: ☐   Clean Litter: ☐   Other:

Billing

Fee Per Visit:	Visits:	Visit Total:
Extra Fees:	Discounts:	Extras Total:
Paid?	Method:	**TOTAL:**

Notes

_____
_____
_____

Pet Name:

Owner

Name:	
Address:	
Email:	Emergency:

Veterinarian

Name:	Phone:

Act Immediately in Emergency: ☐   Contact Owners First: ☐

Pet Info

Nickname:	Age & Gender:
Species:	Breed:
Hiding Places:	Favorite Toy:
Allergies:	Favorite Treat:

Meals

Time:	Meal:	Quantity:
Time:	Meal:	Quantity:
Time:	Meal:	Quantity:

Other

Walk: ☐   Groom: ☐   Play: ☐   Clean Litter: ☐   Other:

Billing

Fee Per Visit:	Visits:	Visit Total:
Extra Fees:	Discounts:	Extras Total:
Paid?	Method:	**TOTAL:**

Notes

_____

_____

_____

_____

Pet Name:

Owner

Name:	
Address:	
Email:	Emergency:

Veterinarian

Name:	Phone:
Act Immediately in Emergency: ☐	Contact Owners First: ☐

Pet Info

Nickname:	Age & Gender:
Species:	Breed:
Hiding Places:	Favorite Toy:
Allergies:	Favorite Treat:

Meals

Time:	Meal:	Quantity:
Time:	Meal:	Quantity:
Time:	Meal:	Quantity:

Other

Walk: ☐   Groom: ☐   Play: ☐   Clean Litter: ☐   Other:

Billing

Fee Per Visit:	Visits:	Visit Total:
Extra Fees:	Discounts:	Extras Total:
Paid?	Method:	**TOTAL:**

Notes

Pet Name:

Owner

Name:

Address:

Email:	Emergency:

Veterinarian

Name:	Phone:

Act Immediately in Emergency: ☐   Contact Owners First: ☐

Pet Info

Nickname:	Age & Gender:
Species:	Breed:
Hiding Places:	Favorite Toy:
Allergies:	Favorite Treat:

Meals

Time:	Meal:	Quantity:
Time:	Meal:	Quantity:
Time:	Meal:	Quantity:

Other

Walk: ☐   Groom: ☐   Play: ☐   Clean Litter: ☐   Other:

Billing

Fee Per Visit:	Visits:	Visit Total:
Extra Fees:	Discounts:	Extras Total:
Paid?	Method:	**TOTAL:**

Notes

Pet Name:

Owner

Name:	
Address:	
Email:	Emergency:

Veterinarian

Name:	Phone:
Act Immediately in Emergency: ☐	Contact Owners First: ☐

Pet Info

Nickname:	Age & Gender:
Species:	Breed:
Hiding Places:	Favorite Toy:
Allergies:	Favorite Treat:

Meals

Time:	Meal:	Quantity:
Time:	Meal:	Quantity:
Time:	Meal:	Quantity:

Other

Walk: ☐   Groom: ☐   Play: ☐   Clean Litter: ☐   Other:

Billing

Fee Per Visit:	Visits:	Visit Total:
Extra Fees:	Discounts:	Extras Total:
Paid?	Method:	**TOTAL:**

Notes

Pet Name:

Owner

Name:

Address:

Email:	Emergency:

Veterinarian

Name:	Phone:

Act Immediately in Emergency: ☐   Contact Owners First: ☐

Pet Info

Nickname:	Age & Gender:
Species:	Breed:
Hiding Places:	Favorite Toy:
Allergies:	Favorite Treat:

Meals

Time:	Meal:	Quantity:
Time:	Meal:	Quantity:
Time:	Meal:	Quantity:

Other

Walk: ☐   Groom: ☐   Play: ☐   Clean Litter: ☐   Other:

Billing

Fee Per Visit:	Visits:	Visit Total:
Extra Fees:	Discounts:	Extras Total:
Paid?	Method:	**TOTAL:**

Notes

NOTES

NOTES

NOTES

NOTES

NOTES

NOTES

NOTES

NOTES

NOTES

NOTES

NOTES

NOTES

NOTES

Month:

Date:							
	MONDAY	**TUESDAY**	**WEDNESDAY**	**THURSDAY**	**FRIDAY**	**SATURDAY**	**SUNDAY**
5:00							
5:30							
6:00							
6:30							
7:00							
7:30							
8:00							
8:30							
9:00							
9:30							
10:00							
10:30							
11:00							
11:30							
12:00							
12:30							
1:00							
1:30							
2:00							
2:30							
3:00							
3:30							
4:00							
4:30							
5:00							
5:30							
6:00							
6:30							
7:00							
7:30							
8:00							
8:30							
9:00							
9:30							
10:00							
10:30							

Month:

Date:							
	MONDAY	**TUESDAY**	**WEDNESDAY**	**THURSDAY**	**FRIDAY**	**SATURDAY**	**SUNDAY**
5:00							
5:30							
6:00							
6:30							
7:00							
7:30							
8:00							
8:30							
9:00							
9:30							
10:00							
10:30							
11:00							
11:30							
12:00							
12:30							
1:00							
1:30							
2:00							
2:30							
3:00							
3:30							
4:00							
4:30							
5:00							
5:30							
6:00							
6:30							
7:00							
7:30							
8:00							
8:30							
9:00							
9:30							
10:00							
10:30							

Month:

Date:							
	MONDAY	TUESDAY	WEDNESDAY	THURSDAY	FRIDAY	SATURDAY	SUNDAY
5:00							
5:30							
6:00							
6:30							
7:00							
7:30							
8:00							
8:30							
9:00							
9:30							
10:00							
10:30							
11:00							
11:30							
12:00							
12:30							
1:00							
1:30							
2:00							
2:30							
3:00							
3:30							
4:00							
4:30							
5:00							
5:30							
6:00							
6:30							
7:00							
7:30							
8:00							
8:30							
9:00							
9:30							
10:00							
10:30							

Month:

Date:							
	MONDAY	**TUESDAY**	**WEDNESDAY**	**THURSDAY**	**FRIDAY**	**SATURDAY**	**SUNDAY**
5:00							
5:30							
6:00							
6:30							
7:00							
7:30							
8:00							
8:30							
9:00							
9:30							
10:00							
10:30							
11:00							
11:30							
12:00							
12:30							
1:00							
1:30							
2:00							
2:30							
3:00							
3:30							
4:00							
4:30							
5:00							
5:30							
6:00							
6:30							
7:00							
7:30							
8:00							
8:30							
9:00							
9:30							
10:00							
10:30							

Month:

Date:							
	MONDAY	**TUESDAY**	**WEDNESDAY**	**THURSDAY**	**FRIDAY**	**SATURDAY**	**SUNDAY**
5:00							
5:30							
6:00							
6:30							
7:00							
7:30							
8:00							
8:30							
9:00							
9:30							
10:00							
10:30							
11:00							
11:30							
12:00							
12:30							
1:00							
1:30							
2:00							
2:30							
3:00							
3:30							
4:00							
4:30							
5:00							
5:30							
6:00							
6:30							
7:00							
7:30							
8:00							
8:30							
9:00							
9:30							
10:00							
10:30							

Month:

Date:							
	MONDAY	**TUESDAY**	**WEDNESDAY**	**THURSDAY**	**FRIDAY**	**SATURDAY**	**SUNDAY**
5:00							
5:30							
6:00							
6:30							
7:00							
7:30							
8:00							
8:30							
9:00							
9:30							
10:00							
10:30							
11:00							
11:30							
12:00							
12:30							
1:00							
1:30							
2:00							
2:30							
3:00							
3:30							
4:00							
4:30							
5:00							
5:30							
6:00							
6:30							
7:00							
7:30							
8:00							
8:30							
9:00							
9:30							
10:00							
10:30							

Month:

Date:							
	MONDAY	**TUESDAY**	**WEDNESDAY**	**THURSDAY**	**FRIDAY**	**SATURDAY**	**SUNDAY**
5:00							
5:30							
6:00							
6:30							
7:00							
7:30							
8:00							
8:30							
9:00							
9:30							
10:00							
10:30							
11:00							
11:30							
12:00							
12:30							
1:00							
1:30							
2:00							
2:30							
3:00							
3:30							
4:00							
4:30							
5:00							
5:30							
6:00							
6:30							
7:00							
7:30							
8:00							
8:30							
9:00							
9:30							
10:00							
10:30							

Month:

Date:							
	MONDAY	**TUESDAY**	**WEDNESDAY**	**THURSDAY**	**FRIDAY**	**SATURDAY**	**SUNDAY**
5:00							
5:30							
6:00							
6:30							
7:00							
7:30							
8:00							
8:30							
9:00							
9:30							
10:00							
10:30							
11:00							
11:30							
12:00							
12:30							
1:00							
1:30							
2:00							
2:30							
3:00							
3:30							
4:00							
4:30							
5:00							
5:30							
6:00							
6:30							
7:00							
7:30							
8:00							
8:30							
9:00							
9:30							
10:00							
10:30							

Month:

Date:							
	MONDAY	**TUESDAY**	**WEDNESDAY**	**THURSDAY**	**FRIDAY**	**SATURDAY**	**SUNDAY**
5:00							
5:30							
6:00							
6:30							
7:00							
7:30							
8:00							
8:30							
9:00							
9:30							
10:00							
10:30							
11:00							
11:30							
12:00							
12:30							
1:00							
1:30							
2:00							
2:30							
3:00							
3:30							
4:00							
4:30							
5:00							
5:30							
6:00							
6:30							
7:00							
7:30							
8:00							
8:30							
9:00							
9:30							
10:00							
10:30							

Month:

Date:							
	MONDAY	**TUESDAY**	**WEDNESDAY**	**THURSDAY**	**FRIDAY**	**SATURDAY**	**SUNDAY**
5:00							
5:30							
6:00							
6:30							
7:00							
7:30							
8:00							
8:30							
9:00							
9:30							
10:00							
10:30							
11:00							
11:30							
12:00							
12:30							
1:00							
1:30							
2:00							
2:30							
3:00							
3:30							
4:00							
4:30							
5:00							
5:30							
6:00							
6:30							
7:00							
7:30							
8:00							
8:30							
9:00							
9:30							
10:00							
10:30							

Month:

Date:							
	MONDAY	**TUESDAY**	**WEDNESDAY**	**THURSDAY**	**FRIDAY**	**SATURDAY**	**SUNDAY**
5:00							
5:30							
6:00							
6:30							
7:00							
7:30							
8:00							
8:30							
9:00							
9:30							
10:00							
10:30							
11:00							
11:30							
12:00							
12:30							
1:00							
1:30							
2:00							
2:30							
3:00							
3:30							
4:00							
4:30							
5:00							
5:30							
6:00							
6:30							
7:00							
7:30							
8:00							
8:30							
9:00							
9:30							
10:00							
10:30							

Month:

Date:							
	MONDAY	**TUESDAY**	**WEDNESDAY**	**THURSDAY**	**FRIDAY**	**SATURDAY**	**SUNDAY**
5:00							
5:30							
6:00							
6:30							
7:00							
7:30							
8:00							
8:30							
9:00							
9:30							
10:00							
10:30							
11:00							
11:30							
12:00							
12:30							
1:00							
1:30							
2:00							
2:30							
3:00							
3:30							
4:00							
4:30							
5:00							
5:30							
6:00							
6:30							
7:00							
7:30							
8:00							
8:30							
9:00							
9:30							
10:00							
10:30							

Month:

Date:							
	MONDAY	**TUESDAY**	**WEDNESDAY**	**THURSDAY**	**FRIDAY**	**SATURDAY**	**SUNDAY**
5:00							
5:30							
6:00							
6:30							
7:00							
7:30							
8:00							
8:30							
9:00							
9:30							
10:00							
10:30							
11:00							
11:30							
12:00							
12:30							
1:00							
1:30							
2:00							
2:30							
3:00							
3:30							
4:00							
4:30							
5:00							
5:30							
6:00							
6:30							
7:00							
7:30							
8:00							
8:30							
9:00							
9:30							
10:00							
10:30							

Month:

Date:							
	MONDAY	**TUESDAY**	**WEDNESDAY**	**THURSDAY**	**FRIDAY**	**SATURDAY**	**SUNDAY**
5:00							
5:30							
6:00							
6:30							
7:00							
7:30							
8:00							
8:30							
9:00							
9:30							
10:00							
10:30							
11:00							
11:30							
12:00							
12:30							
1:00							
1:30							
2:00							
2:30							
3:00							
3:30							
4:00							
4:30							
5:00							
5:30							
6:00							
6:30							
7:00							
7:30							
8:00							
8:30							
9:00							
9:30							
10:00							
10:30							

Month:

Date:							
	MONDAY	**TUESDAY**	**WEDNESDAY**	**THURSDAY**	**FRIDAY**	**SATURDAY**	**SUNDAY**
5:00							
5:30							
6:00							
6:30							
7:00							
7:30							
8:00							
8:30							
9:00							
9:30							
10:00							
10:30							
11:00							
11:30							
12:00							
12:30							
1:00							
1:30							
2:00							
2:30							
3:00							
3:30							
4:00							
4:30							
5:00							
5:30							
6:00							
6:30							
7:00							
7:30							
8:00							
8:30							
9:00							
9:30							
10:00							
10:30							

Month:

Date:							
	MONDAY	**TUESDAY**	**WEDNESDAY**	**THURSDAY**	**FRIDAY**	**SATURDAY**	**SUNDAY**
5:00							
5:30							
6:00							
6:30							
7:00							
7:30							
8:00							
8:30							
9:00							
9:30							
10:00							
10:30							
11:00							
11:30							
12:00							
12:30							
1:00							
1:30							
2:00							
2:30							
3:00							
3:30							
4:00							
4:30							
5:00							
5:30							
6:00							
6:30							
7:00							
7:30							
8:00							
8:30							
9:00							
9:30							
10:00							
10:30							

Month:

Date:							
	MONDAY	**TUESDAY**	**WEDNESDAY**	**THURSDAY**	**FRIDAY**	**SATURDAY**	**SUNDAY**
5:00							
5:30							
6:00							
6:30							
7:00							
7:30							
8:00							
8:30							
9:00							
9:30							
10:00							
10:30							
11:00							
11:30							
12:00							
12:30							
1:00							
1:30							
2:00							
2:30							
3:00							
3:30							
4:00							
4:30							
5:00							
5:30							
6:00							
6:30							
7:00							
7:30							
8:00							
8:30							
9:00							
9:30							
10:00							
10:30							

Month:

Date:							
	MONDAY	**TUESDAY**	**WEDNESDAY**	**THURSDAY**	**FRIDAY**	**SATURDAY**	**SUNDAY**
5:00							
5:30							
6:00							
6:30							
7:00							
7:30							
8:00							
8:30							
9:00							
9:30							
10:00							
10:30							
11:00							
11:30							
12:00							
12:30							
1:00							
1:30							
2:00							
2:30							
3:00							
3:30							
4:00							
4:30							
5:00							
5:30							
6:00							
6:30							
7:00							
7:30							
8:00							
8:30							
9:00							
9:30							
10:00							
10:30							

Month:

Date:							
	MONDAY	**TUESDAY**	**WEDNESDAY**	**THURSDAY**	**FRIDAY**	**SATURDAY**	**SUNDAY**
5:00							
5:30							
6:00							
6:30							
7:00							
7:30							
8:00							
8:30							
9:00							
9:30							
10:00							
10:30							
11:00							
11:30							
12:00							
12:30							
1:00							
1:30							
2:00							
2:30							
3:00							
3:30							
4:00							
4:30							
5:00							
5:30							
6:00							
6:30							
7:00							
7:30							
8:00							
8:30							
9:00							
9:30							
10:00							
10:30							

Month:

Date:	MONDAY	TUESDAY	WEDNESDAY	THURSDAY	FRIDAY	SATURDAY	SUNDAY
5:00							
5:30							
6:00							
6:30							
7:00							
7:30							
8:00							
8:30							
9:00							
9:30							
10:00							
10:30							
11:00							
11:30							
12:00							
12:30							
1:00							
1:30							
2:00							
2:30							
3:00							
3:30							
4:00							
4:30							
5:00							
5:30							
6:00							
6:30							
7:00							
7:30							
8:00							
8:30							
9:00							
9:30							
10:00							
10:30							

Month:

Date:							
	MONDAY	**TUESDAY**	**WEDNESDAY**	**THURSDAY**	**FRIDAY**	**SATURDAY**	**SUNDAY**
5:00							
5:30							
6:00							
6:30							
7:00							
7:30							
8:00							
8:30							
9:00							
9:30							
10:00							
10:30							
11:00							
11:30							
12:00							
12:30							
1:00							
1:30							
2:00							
2:30							
3:00							
3:30							
4:00							
4:30							
5:00							
5:30							
6:00							
6:30							
7:00							
7:30							
8:00							
8:30							
9:00							
9:30							
10:00							
10:30							

Month:

Date:							
	MONDAY	**TUESDAY**	**WEDNESDAY**	**THURSDAY**	**FRIDAY**	**SATURDAY**	**SUNDAY**
5:00							
5:30							
6:00							
6:30							
7:00							
7:30							
8:00							
8:30							
9:00							
9:30							
10:00							
10:30							
11:00							
11:30							
12:00							
12:30							
1:00							
1:30							
2:00							
2:30							
3:00							
3:30							
4:00							
4:30							
5:00							
5:30							
6:00							
6:30							
7:00							
7:30							
8:00							
8:30							
9:00							
9:30							
10:00							
10:30							

Month:

Date:							
	MONDAY	**TUESDAY**	**WEDNESDAY**	**THURSDAY**	**FRIDAY**	**SATURDAY**	**SUNDAY**
5:00							
5:30							
6:00							
6:30							
7:00							
7:30							
8:00							
8:30							
9:00							
9:30							
10:00							
10:30							
11:00							
11:30							
12:00							
12:30							
1:00							
1:30							
2:00							
2:30							
3:00							
3:30							
4:00							
4:30							
5:00							
5:30							
6:00							
6:30							
7:00							
7:30							
8:00							
8:30							
9:00							
9:30							
10:00							
10:30							

Month:

Date:							
	MONDAY	**TUESDAY**	**WEDNESDAY**	**THURSDAY**	**FRIDAY**	**SATURDAY**	**SUNDAY**
5:00							
5:30							
6:00							
6:30							
7:00							
7:30							
8:00							
8:30							
9:00							
9:30							
10:00							
10:30							
11:00							
11:30							
12:00							
12:30							
1:00							
1:30							
2:00							
2:30							
3:00							
3:30							
4:00							
4:30							
5:00							
5:30							
6:00							
6:30							
7:00							
7:30							
8:00							
8:30							
9:00							
9:30							
10:00							
10:30							

Month:

Date:							
	MONDAY	**TUESDAY**	**WEDNESDAY**	**THURSDAY**	**FRIDAY**	**SATURDAY**	**SUNDAY**
5:00							
5:30							
6:00							
6:30							
7:00							
7:30							
8:00							
8:30							
9:00							
9:30							
10:00							
10:30							
11:00							
11:30							
12:00							
12:30							
1:00							
1:30							
2:00							
2:30							
3:00							
3:30							
4:00							
4:30							
5:00							
5:30							
6:00							
6:30							
7:00							
7:30							
8:00							
8:30							
9:00							
9:30							
10:00							
10:30							

Month:

Date:							
	MONDAY	**TUESDAY**	**WEDNESDAY**	**THURSDAY**	**FRIDAY**	**SATURDAY**	**SUNDAY**
5:00							
5:30							
6:00							
6:30							
7:00							
7:30							
8:00							
8:30							
9:00							
9:30							
10:00							
10:30							
11:00							
11:30							
12:00							
12:30							
1:00							
1:30							
2:00							
2:30							
3:00							
3:30							
4:00							
4:30							
5:00							
5:30							
6:00							
6:30							
7:00							
7:30							
8:00							
8:30							
9:00							
9:30							
10:00							
10:30							

Month:

Date:							
	MONDAY	**TUESDAY**	**WEDNESDAY**	**THURSDAY**	**FRIDAY**	**SATURDAY**	**SUNDAY**
5:00							
5:30							
6:00							
6:30							
7:00							
7:30							
8:00							
8:30							
9:00							
9:30							
10:00							
10:30							
11:00							
11:30							
12:00							
12:30							
1:00							
1:30							
2:00							
2:30							
3:00							
3:30							
4:00							
4:30							
5:00							
5:30							
6:00							
6:30							
7:00							
7:30							
8:00							
8:30							
9:00							
9:30							
10:00							
10:30							

Month:

Date:							
	MONDAY	**TUESDAY**	**WEDNESDAY**	**THURSDAY**	**FRIDAY**	**SATURDAY**	**SUNDAY**
5:00							
5:30							
6:00							
6:30							
7:00							
7:30							
8:00							
8:30							
9:00							
9:30							
10:00							
10:30							
11:00							
11:30							
12:00							
12:30							
1:00							
1:30							
2:00							
2:30							
3:00							
3:30							
4:00							
4:30							
5:00							
5:30							
6:00							
6:30							
7:00							
7:30							
8:00							
8:30							
9:00							
9:30							
10:00							
10:30							

Month:

Date:							
	MONDAY	**TUESDAY**	**WEDNESDAY**	**THURSDAY**	**FRIDAY**	**SATURDAY**	**SUNDAY**
5:00							
5:30							
6:00							
6:30							
7:00							
7:30							
8:00							
8:30							
9:00							
9:30							
10:00							
10:30							
11:00							
11:30							
12:00							
12:30							
1:00							
1:30							
2:00							
2:30							
3:00							
3:30							
4:00							
4:30							
5:00							
5:30							
6:00							
6:30							
7:00							
7:30							
8:00							
8:30							
9:00							
9:30							
10:00							
10:30							

Month:

Date:							
	MONDAY	**TUESDAY**	**WEDNESDAY**	**THURSDAY**	**FRIDAY**	**SATURDAY**	**SUNDAY**
5:00							
5:30							
6:00							
6:30							
7:00							
7:30							
8:00							
8:30							
9:00							
9:30							
10:00							
10:30							
11:00							
11:30							
12:00							
12:30							
1:00							
1:30							
2:00							
2:30							
3:00							
3:30							
4:00							
4:30							
5:00							
5:30							
6:00							
6:30							
7:00							
7:30							
8:00							
8:30							
9:00							
9:30							
10:00							
10:30							

Month:

Date:							
	MONDAY	**TUESDAY**	**WEDNESDAY**	**THURSDAY**	**FRIDAY**	**SATURDAY**	**SUNDAY**
5:00							
5:30							
6:00							
6:30							
7:00							
7:30							
8:00							
8:30							
9:00							
9:30							
10:00							
10:30							
11:00							
11:30							
12:00							
12:30							
1:00							
1:30							
2:00							
2:30							
3:00							
3:30							
4:00							
4:30							
5:00							
5:30							
6:00							
6:30							
7:00							
7:30							
8:00							
8:30							
9:00							
9:30							
10:00							
10:30							

Month:

Date:	MONDAY	TUESDAY	WEDNESDAY	THURSDAY	FRIDAY	SATURDAY	SUNDAY
5:00							
5:30							
6:00							
6:30							
7:00							
7:30							
8:00							
8:30							
9:00							
9:30							
10:00							
10:30							
11:00							
11:30							
12:00							
12:30							
1:00							
1:30							
2:00							
2:30							
3:00							
3:30							
4:00							
4:30							
5:00							
5:30							
6:00							
6:30							
7:00							
7:30							
8:00							
8:30							
9:00							
9:30							
10:00							
10:30							

Month:

Date:							
	MONDAY	**TUESDAY**	**WEDNESDAY**	**THURSDAY**	**FRIDAY**	**SATURDAY**	**SUNDAY**
5:00							
5:30							
6:00							
6:30							
7:00							
7:30							
8:00							
8:30							
9:00							
9:30							
10:00							
10:30							
11:00							
11:30							
12:00							
12:30							
1:00							
1:30							
2:00							
2:30							
3:00							
3:30							
4:00							
4:30							
5:00							
5:30							
6:00							
6:30							
7:00							
7:30							
8:00							
8:30							
9:00							
9:30							
10:00							
10:30							

Month:

Date:							
	MONDAY	**TUESDAY**	**WEDNESDAY**	**THURSDAY**	**FRIDAY**	**SATURDAY**	**SUNDAY**
5:00							
5:30							
6:00							
6:30							
7:00							
7:30							
8:00							
8:30							
9:00							
9:30							
10:00							
10:30							
11:00							
11:30							
12:00							
12:30							
1:00							
1:30							
2:00							
2:30							
3:00							
3:30							
4:00							
4:30							
5:00							
5:30							
6:00							
6:30							
7:00							
7:30							
8:00							
8:30							
9:00							
9:30							
10:00							
10:30							

Month:

Date:							
	MONDAY	**TUESDAY**	**WEDNESDAY**	**THURSDAY**	**FRIDAY**	**SATURDAY**	**SUNDAY**
5:00							
5:30							
6:00							
6:30							
7:00							
7:30							
8:00							
8:30							
9:00							
9:30							
10:00							
10:30							
11:00							
11:30							
12:00							
12:30							
1:00							
1:30							
2:00							
2:30							
3:00							
3:30							
4:00							
4:30							
5:00							
5:30							
6:00							
6:30							
7:00							
7:30							
8:00							
8:30							
9:00							
9:30							
10:00							
10:30							

Month:

Date:	MONDAY	TUESDAY	WEDNESDAY	THURSDAY	FRIDAY	SATURDAY	SUNDAY
5:00							
5:30							
6:00							
6:30							
7:00							
7:30							
8:00							
8:30							
9:00							
9:30							
10:00							
10:30							
11:00							
11:30							
12:00							
12:30							
1:00							
1:30							
2:00							
2:30							
3:00							
3:30							
4:00							
4:30							
5:00							
5:30							
6:00							
6:30							
7:00							
7:30							
8:00							
8:30							
9:00							
9:30							
10:00							
10:30							

Month:

Date:							
	MONDAY	**TUESDAY**	**WEDNESDAY**	**THURSDAY**	**FRIDAY**	**SATURDAY**	**SUNDAY**
5:00							
5:30							
6:00							
6:30							
7:00							
7:30							
8:00							
8:30							
9:00							
9:30							
10:00							
10:30							
11:00							
11:30							
12:00							
12:30							
1:00							
1:30							
2:00							
2:30							
3:00							
3:30							
4:00							
4:30							
5:00							
5:30							
6:00							
6:30							
7:00							
7:30							
8:00							
8:30							
9:00							
9:30							
10:00							
10:30							

Month:

Date:							
	MONDAY	**TUESDAY**	**WEDNESDAY**	**THURSDAY**	**FRIDAY**	**SATURDAY**	**SUNDAY**
5:00							
5:30							
6:00							
6:30							
7:00							
7:30							
8:00							
8:30							
9:00							
9:30							
10:00							
10:30							
11:00							
11:30							
12:00							
12:30							
1:00							
1:30							
2:00							
2:30							
3:00							
3:30							
4:00							
4:30							
5:00							
5:30							
6:00							
6:30							
7:00							
7:30							
8:00							
8:30							
9:00							
9:30							
10:00							
10:30							

Month:

Date:							
	MONDAY	**TUESDAY**	**WEDNESDAY**	**THURSDAY**	**FRIDAY**	**SATURDAY**	**SUNDAY**
5:00							
5:30							
6:00							
6:30							
7:00							
7:30							
8:00							
8:30							
9:00							
9:30							
10:00							
10:30							
11:00							
11:30							
12:00							
12:30							
1:00							
1:30							
2:00							
2:30							
3:00							
3:30							
4:00							
4:30							
5:00							
5:30							
6:00							
6:30							
7:00							
7:30							
8:00							
8:30							
9:00							
9:30							
10:00							
10:30							

Month:

Date:							
	MONDAY	**TUESDAY**	**WEDNESDAY**	**THURSDAY**	**FRIDAY**	**SATURDAY**	**SUNDAY**
5:00							
5:30							
6:00							
6:30							
7:00							
7:30							
8:00							
8:30							
9:00							
9:30							
10:00							
10:30							
11:00							
11:30							
12:00							
12:30							
1:00							
1:30							
2:00							
2:30							
3:00							
3:30							
4:00							
4:30							
5:00							
5:30							
6:00							
6:30							
7:00							
7:30							
8:00							
8:30							
9:00							
9:30							
10:00							
10:30							

Month:

Date:							
	MONDAY	**TUESDAY**	**WEDNESDAY**	**THURSDAY**	**FRIDAY**	**SATURDAY**	**SUNDAY**
5:00							
5:30							
6:00							
6:30							
7:00							
7:30							
8:00							
8:30							
9:00							
9:30							
10:00							
10:30							
11:00							
11:30							
12:00							
12:30							
1:00							
1:30							
2:00							
2:30							
3:00							
3:30							
4:00							
4:30							
5:00							
5:30							
6:00							
6:30							
7:00							
7:30							
8:00							
8:30							
9:00							
9:30							
10:00							
10:30							

Month:

Date:							
	MONDAY	**TUESDAY**	**WEDNESDAY**	**THURSDAY**	**FRIDAY**	**SATURDAY**	**SUNDAY**
5:00							
5:30							
6:00							
6:30							
7:00							
7:30							
8:00							
8:30							
9:00							
9:30							
10:00							
10:30							
11:00							
11:30							
12:00							
12:30							
1:00							
1:30							
2:00							
2:30							
3:00							
3:30							
4:00							
4:30							
5:00							
5:30							
6:00							
6:30							
7:00							
7:30							
8:00							
8:30							
9:00							
9:30							
10:00							
10:30							

Month:

Date:							
	MONDAY	**TUESDAY**	**WEDNESDAY**	**THURSDAY**	**FRIDAY**	**SATURDAY**	**SUNDAY**
5:00							
5:30							
6:00							
6:30							
7:00							
7:30							
8:00							
8:30							
9:00							
9:30							
10:00							
10:30							
11:00							
11:30							
12:00							
12:30							
1:00							
1:30							
2:00							
2:30							
3:00							
3:30							
4:00							
4:30							
5:00							
5:30							
6:00							
6:30							
7:00							
7:30							
8:00							
8:30							
9:00							
9:30							
10:00							
10:30							

Month:

Date:							
	MONDAY	**TUESDAY**	**WEDNESDAY**	**THURSDAY**	**FRIDAY**	**SATURDAY**	**SUNDAY**
5:00							
5:30							
6:00							
6:30							
7:00							
7:30							
8:00							
8:30							
9:00							
9:30							
10:00							
10:30							
11:00							
11:30							
12:00							
12:30							
1:00							
1:30							
2:00							
2:30							
3:00							
3:30							
4:00							
4:30							
5:00							
5:30							
6:00							
6:30							
7:00							
7:30							
8:00							
8:30							
9:00							
9:30							
10:00							
10:30							

Month:

Date:							
	MONDAY	**TUESDAY**	**WEDNESDAY**	**THURSDAY**	**FRIDAY**	**SATURDAY**	**SUNDAY**
5:00							
5:30							
6:00							
6:30							
7:00							
7:30							
8:00							
8:30							
9:00							
9:30							
10:00							
10:30							
11:00							
11:30							
12:00							
12:30							
1:00							
1:30							
2:00							
2:30							
3:00							
3:30							
4:00							
4:30							
5:00							
5:30							
6:00							
6:30							
7:00							
7:30							
8:00							
8:30							
9:00							
9:30							
10:00							
10:30							

Month:

Date:							
	MONDAY	**TUESDAY**	**WEDNESDAY**	**THURSDAY**	**FRIDAY**	**SATURDAY**	**SUNDAY**
5:00							
5:30							
6:00							
6:30							
7:00							
7:30							
8:00							
8:30							
9:00							
9:30							
10:00							
10:30							
11:00							
11:30							
12:00							
12:30							
1:00							
1:30							
2:00							
2:30							
3:00							
3:30							
4:00							
4:30							
5:00							
5:30							
6:00							
6:30							
7:00							
7:30							
8:00							
8:30							
9:00							
9:30							
10:00							
10:30							

Month:

Date:							
	MONDAY	**TUESDAY**	**WEDNESDAY**	**THURSDAY**	**FRIDAY**	**SATURDAY**	**SUNDAY**
5:00							
5:30							
6:00							
6:30							
7:00							
7:30							
8:00							
8:30							
9:00							
9:30							
10:00							
10:30							
11:00							
11:30							
12:00							
12:30							
1:00							
1:30							
2:00							
2:30							
3:00							
3:30							
4:00							
4:30							
5:00							
5:30							
6:00							
6:30							
7:00							
7:30							
8:00							
8:30							
9:00							
9:30							
10:00							
10:30							

Month:

Date:							
	MONDAY	**TUESDAY**	**WEDNESDAY**	**THURSDAY**	**FRIDAY**	**SATURDAY**	**SUNDAY**
5:00							
5:30							
6:00							
6:30							
7:00							
7:30							
8:00							
8:30							
9:00							
9:30							
10:00							
10:30							
11:00							
11:30							
12:00							
12:30							
1:00							
1:30							
2:00							
2:30							
3:00							
3:30							
4:00							
4:30							
5:00							
5:30							
6:00							
6:30							
7:00							
7:30							
8:00							
8:30							
9:00							
9:30							
10:00							
10:30							

Month:

Date:							
	MONDAY	**TUESDAY**	**WEDNESDAY**	**THURSDAY**	**FRIDAY**	**SATURDAY**	**SUNDAY**
5:00							
5:30							
6:00							
6:30							
7:00							
7:30							
8:00							
8:30							
9:00							
9:30							
10:00							
10:30							
11:00							
11:30							
12:00							
12:30							
1:00							
1:30							
2:00							
2:30							
3:00							
3:30							
4:00							
4:30							
5:00							
5:30							
6:00							
6:30							
7:00							
7:30							
8:00							
8:30							
9:00							
9:30							
10:00							
10:30							

Month:

Date:							
	MONDAY	**TUESDAY**	**WEDNESDAY**	**THURSDAY**	**FRIDAY**	**SATURDAY**	**SUNDAY**
5:00							
5:30							
6:00							
6:30							
7:00							
7:30							
8:00							
8:30							
9:00							
9:30							
10:00							
10:30							
11:00							
11:30							
12:00							
12:30							
1:00							
1:30							
2:00							
2:30							
3:00							
3:30							
4:00							
4:30							
5:00							
5:30							
6:00							
6:30							
7:00							
7:30							
8:00							
8:30							
9:00							
9:30							
10:00							
10:30							

Month:

Date:							
	MONDAY	**TUESDAY**	**WEDNESDAY**	**THURSDAY**	**FRIDAY**	**SATURDAY**	**SUNDAY**
5:00							
5:30							
6:00							
6:30							
7:00							
7:30							
8:00							
8:30							
9:00							
9:30							
10:00							
10:30							
11:00							
11:30							
12:00							
12:30							
1:00							
1:30							
2:00							
2:30							
3:00							
3:30							
4:00							
4:30							
5:00							
5:30							
6:00							
6:30							
7:00							
7:30							
8:00							
8:30							
9:00							
9:30							
10:00							
10:30							

Month:

Date:							
	MONDAY	**TUESDAY**	**WEDNESDAY**	**THURSDAY**	**FRIDAY**	**SATURDAY**	**SUNDAY**
5:00							
5:30							
6:00							
6:30							
7:00							
7:30							
8:00							
8:30							
9:00							
9:30							
10:00							
10:30							
11:00							
11:30							
12:00							
12:30							
1:00							
1:30							
2:00							
2:30							
3:00							
3:30							
4:00							
4:30							
5:00							
5:30							
6:00							
6:30							
7:00							
7:30							
8:00							
8:30							
9:00							
9:30							
10:00							
10:30							

Made in the USA
Las Vegas, NV
24 February 2022